VanderCook Etudes

by H. A. VanderCook

Published for:

*CORNET or TRUMPET

(Baritone Treble Clef — E♭ Alto — Mellophone)

*TROMBONE or BARITONE (Bass Clef)

(Transcribed and Edited by Walter C. Welke)

● E♭ or BB♭ BASS (Tuba)

* B♭ Cornet, Trumpet, Trombone, and Baritone are playable together.

RUBANK® HAL•LEONARD® CORPORATION

7777 W. BLUEMOUND RD. P.O. BOX 13819 MILWAUKEE, WI 53213

Vander Cook Etudes for E♭ or BB♭ Bass

Etude 1

D.C.

Etude 2

D.C.

Copyright, MCM XLI, by Rubank, Inc., Chicago, Ill.
International Copyright Secured

Etude 3

D.C.

Etude 4

D.C.

Etude 5

D.C.

Etude 6

D.C.

Etude 7

D.C.

Etude 8

5

Etude 9

D.C.

Etude 10

6

Etude 11

Etude 12

Etude 13

Etude 14

Etude 15

9

Etude 16

Etude 17

D.C.

Etude 18

D. C.

Etude 19

Etude 20

Etude 21

Etude 22

Etude 23

Etude 24

Etude 25

Etude 26

Etude 27

Etude 28

Etude 29

Etude 30

Etude 31

Etude 32

Etude 33

Etude 34

Etude 35

Etude 36

Etude 37

Etude 38

Etude 39

Etude 40

Etude 41

Etude 42

Etude 43

Etude 44

Etude 45

Etude 46

Andante legato

Etude 47

Grave

Etude 48

Andante legato

Etude 49

Sprightly

Etude 50

Andante legato

Bombastoso

Caprice

VANDER COOK

Etude 51

Copyright, MCMXLI, by Rubank, Inc., Chicago, Ill.
International Copyright Secured

This number available in sheet music form with Piano accompaniment.

Colossus
Air and Variations

Etude 52

VANDER COOK

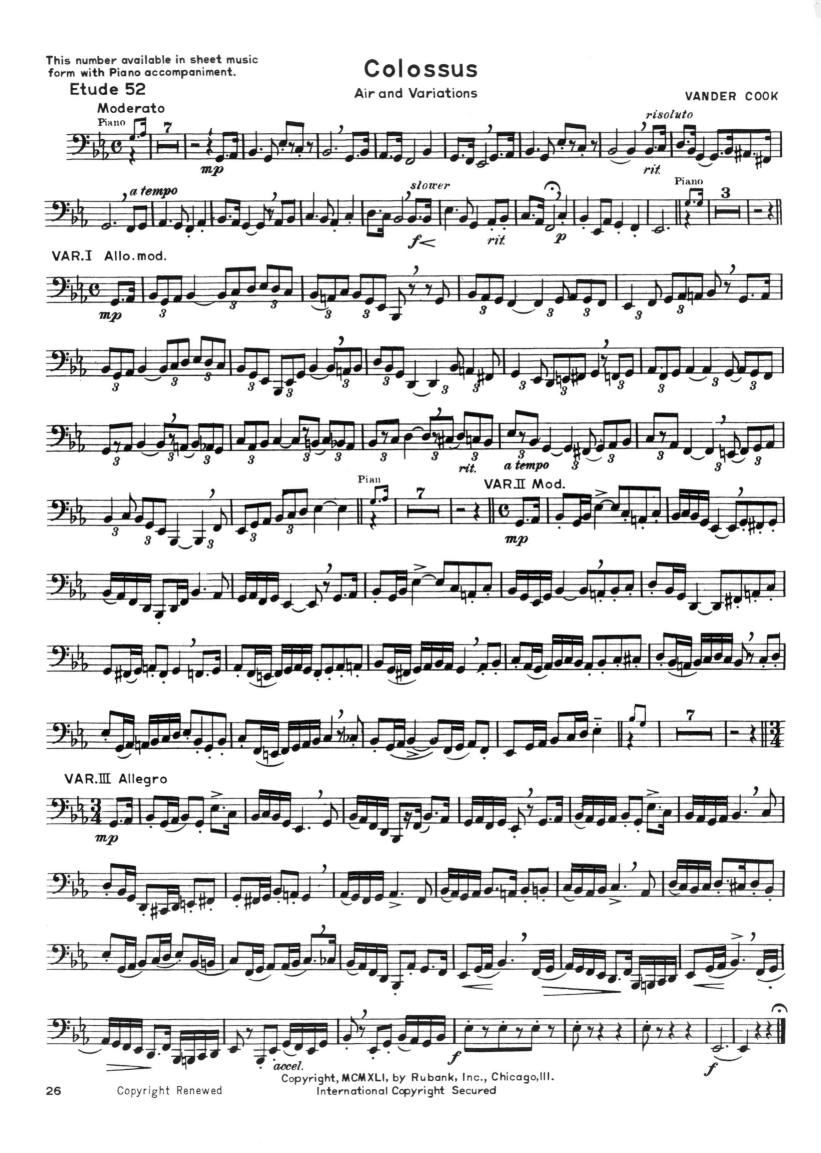